FUNdamental Experiments

Liquids and Solids

by Ellen Lawrence

Consultants:

Suzy Gazlay, MA
Recipient, Presidential Award for Excellence in Science Teaching

Kimberly Brenneman, PhD
National Institute for Early Education Research, Rutgers University, New Brunswick, New Jersey

BEARPORT
PUBLISHING

New York, New York

Credits

Cover, © Kuttelvaserova Stuchelova/Shutterstock and © Feng Yu/Shutterstock; 3, © CoraMax/Shutterstock, © Iakov Filimonov/Shutterstock, and © Valentyn Volkov/Shutterstock; 4, © Gladskikh Tatiana/Shutterstock and © Patrick Foto/Shutterstock; 5, © CoraMax/Shutterstock, © photosync/Shutterstock, © ancroft/Shutterstock, © OneO2/Shutterstock, © Ryan McVay/Thinkstock, and © Asaf Eliason/Shutterstock; 6–7, © CoraMax/Shutterstock, © Ingvar Bjork/Shutterstock, © Planner/Shutterstock, and © Igor Kovalchuk/Shutterstock; 8–9, © CoraMax/Shutterstock and © Coprid/Shutterstock; 10–11, © CoraMax/Shutterstock, © Coprid/Shutterstock, © urfin/Shutterstock, and © Robyn Mackenzie/Shutterstock; 12–13, © CoraMax/Shutterstock, © urfin/Shutterstock, © Thongchai Pittayanon/Shutterstock, © Makaule/Shutterstock, © Asaf Eliason/Shutterstock, © Tim UR/Shutterstock, and © Feng Yu/Shutterstock; 14–15, © CoraMax/Shutterstock, © Tim UR/Shutterstock, © Brian A. Jackson/Shutterstock, © Iakov Filimonov/Shutterstock, © TrotzOlga/Shutterstock, © STILLFX/Shutterstock, and © TrotzOlga/Shutterstock; 16–17, © CoraMax/Shutterstock, © Picsfive/Shutterstock, © Brian A. Jackson/Shutterstock, © Krnetic Vladimir/Shutterstock, © Valentyn Volkov/Shutterstock, © Jack Jelly/Shutterstock, © nexus 7/Shutterstock, © smuay/Shutterstock, and © Margrit Hirsch/Shutterstock; 18–19, © CoraMax/Shutterstock and © artiomp/Shutterstock; 20–21, © CoraMax/Shutterstock, © Valentyn Volkov/Shutterstock, © Iakov Filimonov/Shutterstock, © Planner/Shutterstock, © Igor Kovalchuk/Shutterstock, © Coprid/Shutterstock, © urfin/Shutterstock, © Thongchai Pittayanon/Shutterstock, © Makaule/Shutterstock, © Asaf Eliason/Shutterstock, © Tim UR/Shutterstock, © Feng Yu/Shutterstock, © TrotzOlga/Shutterstock, © Brian A. Jackson/Shutterstock, © nexus 7/Shutterstock, © Jack Jelly/Shutterstock, © Picsfive/Shutterstock, and © artiomp/Shutterstock; 22, © Hung Chung Chih/Shutterstock, © oksana2010/Shutterstock, © Lilya Espinosa/Shutterstock, © mikeledray/Shutterstock, © lightpoet/Shutterstock, and © rmnoa357/Shutterstock; 23, © CoraMax/Shutterstock, © TrotzOlga/Shutterstock, © Africa Studio/Shutterstock, © Tatyana Vyc/Shutterstock, © racorn/Shutterstock, © Valentyn Volkov/Shutterstock, © Robyn Mackenzie/Shutterstock, © Sonya Etchison/Shutterstock, and © Ljupco Smokovski/Shutterstock.

Publisher: Kenn Goin
Senior Editor: Joyce Tavolacci
Creative Director: Spencer Brinker
Design: Emma Randall
Photo Researcher: Ruby Tuesday Books Ltd.

Library of Congress Cataloging-in-Publication Data in process at time of publication (2015)
Library of Congress Control Number: 2014018997
ISBN-13: 978-1-62724-311-7 (library binding)

For more information, write to Bearport Publishing Company, Inc., 45 West 21st Street, Suite 3B, New York, NY 10010. Printed in the United States of America.

10 9 8 7 6 5 4 3 2 1

Contents

Let's Investigate Liquids and Solids

When you are thirsty, you get a glass, fill it with water, and take a sip. You might notice that the glass feels hard. If you pour some water into your hand, however, it **flows** and trickles away. The things you are noticing are different **properties** of the **liquid** water and the **solid** glass. So what properties make something a liquid or a solid? Inside this book are lots of fun experiments and cool facts about liquids and solids. So grab a notebook, and let's start investigating!

Check It Out!

There are liquids and solids all around you. Do you think you can describe what a liquid or a solid is, though? Let's check it out!

What is a liquid?

Fill a cup with water. Use your hand to try to pick up some water out of the cup.

▶ What happens to the water when you try to pick it up? What shape is the water?

Find some plastic containers in your home that are different shapes. Now pour the water out of the cup into the containers. Observe how the water flows and becomes the shape of each container.

What is a solid?

Find a stone, a coin, a pencil eraser, and some plastic containers. Touch and examine the stone, coin, and eraser.

▶ How does each object feel? For example, is it hard or soft, rough or smooth? What shape is it?

Now put each object into a container, one at a time. Then pour each object into a different container.

▶ Did the objects change shape when you moved them from one container to another?

Properties of a Liquid

- A liquid flows.
- A liquid does not have its own shape. It takes the shape of the container it is in.

Properties of a Solid

- A solid does not flow.
- A solid has its own shape. It does not take the shape of the container it is placed in.

5

What happens to liquids when they are mixed together?

All liquids flow and can be poured. What happens to a liquid, though, if it is poured into another liquid and mixed? In this first investigation, you will mix different liquids together to find out. Grab your notebook and a pencil, and let's get mixing!

You will need:

- Three glasses
- Half a cup (118 ml) of apple juice
- Half a cup (118 ml) of milk
- Half a cup (118 ml) of cooking oil
- Blue food coloring
- A jug of water
- A spoon
- A measuring cup
- A notebook and pencil

1 Pour half a cup (118 ml) of apple juice into the first glass. Pour half a cup (118 ml) of milk into the second glass. Then pour half a cup (118 ml) of cooking oil into the third glass.

2 Put five drops of blue food coloring into the jug of water and mix the water with a spoon.

3 Pour half a cup (118 ml) of the blue water into the apple juice. Mix the two liquids together with a spoon.

▶ What happens to the apple juice?

Write your observations in your notebook.

4 Get ready to repeat the same experiment with the milk and then with the oil.

▶ What do you think will happen when each liquid is mixed with the blue water?

Write your **predictions** in your notebook. Then try the experiments and observe what happens.

In your notebook, write down everything you observed.

▶ Did your predictions match what happened?

▶ Did any of the results surprise you?

(To learn more about this investigation and find the answers to the questions, see pages 20–21.)

Which liquid flows the fastest?

Some liquids are thin and watery, while others are thick. A liquid's thickness is called its **viscosity**. The viscosity of a liquid affects how quickly it flows. In this next investigation, you will race some liquids down a sloping tray to find out which one flows the fastest!

You will need:

- Milk
- Ketchup
- Honey
- Shower gel
- Cooking oil
- A notebook and pencil
- A tray
- A spoon
- Paper towels
- A ruler

1 Look at the five liquids you will be testing.

▶ Which liquid do you think is the thinnest?

▶ Which liquid is the thickest?

Write your ideas in your notebook.

2 Now write down the following predictions for the race.

▶ Which liquid will flow the fastest and win the race?

▶ Which one will flow the slowest?

3 Place a tray flat on a table. Put a spoonful of milk at one end of the tray. Wipe the spoon clean with a paper towel. Then repeat the step with the other four liquids, so that all five liquids are in a line.

4 Hold the tray at the end closest to the liquids. Then start the race by slowly tilting the tray until the end is about six inches (15 cm) off the table. Watch the liquids flow down the tray.

Write down the results of the race.

▶ Did your predictions match what happened?

▶ Which liquid has the most viscosity? Which has the least?

(To learn more about this investigation and find the answers to the questions, see pages 20–21.)

GO!

What happens when a liquid gets cold?

Most of the time, liquids are runny and can be poured. Sometimes, however, a liquid can change. In this next investigation, you will discover what happens to some liquids when they are chilled in a freezer. Let's investigate!

You will need:

- An ice cube tray
- A spoon
- Water
- Paper towels
- Milk
- Ketchup
- Cooking oil
- Chocolate sauce
- Shower gel
- Dishwashing liquid
- Vinegar
- A notebook and pencil
- A freezer

 Place an ice cube tray on a table.

 Use a spoon to fill one section of the tray with water. Wipe the spoon clean with a paper towel.

Now repeat this step with the other seven liquids, filling a different section of the tray with a different liquid.

▶ What do you think will happen to the water in the freezer?

▶ What do you think will happen to the other liquids in the freezer?

Write your predictions in your notebook.

 Place the tray in the freezer. Then check the tray after two hours. Examine the liquids.

In your notebook, record everything you observed.

▶ How has the water changed?

▶ How have the other liquids changed?

(To learn more about this investigation and find the answers to the questions, see pages 20–21.)

What happens to a solid when it's put in water?

You've discovered a lot about the properties of liquids. Now it's time to investigate the properties of some solids. In this investigation, you will discover what happens when different solid objects are put into a liquid. What happens to a coin in water, for example? Does the same thing happen to a leaf? Grab your notebook and pencil, and let's find out.

You will need:

- A large bowl
- A large jug of water
- A coin
- A small leaf
- A metal fork
- A rubber band
- A scoop of sand
- Some dry macaroni
- A toothpick
- A stone
- A notebook and pencil

1 Fill a large bowl with water.

2 Place the eight objects you will be testing on a table.

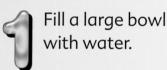

3 Begin by dropping the coin into the bowl of water.

▶ **What does the coin do?**

Now drop the leaf into the water.

▶ **What does the leaf do?**

In your notebook, write down your observations.

4 Closely examine each of the other objects.

▶ **Do you think it will sink like the coin or float like the leaf?**

Draw a chart like this in your notebook.

Objects to be tested	My prediction Sink or float?	Experiment results Sink or float?
Metal fork		
Rubber band		
Sand		
Macaroni		
Toothpick		
Stone		

Record your predictions on the chart. Then test each object and record your results.

▶ Did your predictions match what happened?

▶ What are two of the properties of solids that you discovered in this investigation?

(To learn more about this investigation and find the answers to the questions, see pages 20–21.)

13

Can a solid absorb water?

In the last investigation, you discovered that some solids float when they are put into liquid. Other solids sink, however. What else might happen to a solid when it comes into contact with a liquid? For example, can a solid **absorb**, or soak up, a liquid? Let's investigate!

You will need:

- A small kitchen sponge
- A lump of modeling clay
- A small square of aluminum foil
- A cotton ball
- A large leaf
- A sock
- A small square of thick cardboard
- A plastic block
- A teaspoon
- Water
- A notebook and pencil

1 Place the eight solid objects you will be testing on a table.

2 Carefully pour a teaspoon of water onto the kitchen sponge.

▶ What do you observe happening to the water?

4 Now repeat the experiment by pouring a teaspoon of water onto each of the other objects, one by one.

3 Closely examine the other objects.

▶ Do you think they are absorbent and will soak up the water? Or are they nonabsorbent and won't soak up the water?

In your notebook, write down your predictions.

In your notebook, write down everything you observed.

▶ Did your predictions match what happened?

(To learn more about this investigation and find the answers to the questions, see pages 20–21.)

Can a solid become a liquid?

You've discovered that solids do not flow or change their shape. Is there a way, however, to change a solid so that it turns into a liquid? In this next investigation, you will heat some solids to test if they can be turned into liquids. Let's investigate!

You will need:

- A pencil eraser
- A small lump of modeling clay
- A square of chocolate
- An ice cube
- A cold cube of butter
- A cube of hard cheese
- A notebook and pencil
- Six small tinfoil dishes
- A large baking tray
- An adult helper
- Hot tap water

1 Begin by examining the six solids.

▶ How do they feel in your hands?

▶ How are they similar? How are they different?

▶ Do you think it's possible for each one to change into a liquid?

Write your ideas and predictions in your notebook.

2 Place each of the materials into a separate foil dish.

3 Ask an adult to help you fill a baking tray with hot tap water.

4 Carefully place the six foil dishes in the baking tray. Then observe what happens to each material as it gets warmer.

▶ What did you observe happening to each of the materials?

▶ Which solids changed into liquids?

▶ Did any of them remain solid?

(To learn more about this investigation and find the answers to the questions, see pages 20–21.)

Is it a liquid or a solid?

In this final investigation, you are going to make and test a very mysterious material. Have fun testing the slimy substance, and find out if you can answer the question—is it a liquid or a solid?

You will need:

- Sheets of newspaper
- A large sheet of wax paper
- One cup (237 ml) of cornstarch
- A bowl
- Half a cup (118 ml) of water
- A spoon
- An empty yogurt container
- Paper towels

 Cover a table with newspaper. Place a large sheet of wax paper on top of the newspaper.

 Put the cornstarch into a bowl. Then add the water. Mix the mystery material with a spoon until it is thick and smooth. Now get testing!

 Stir the mystery material with your hands. Scoop up a handful and then hold out your hand so it is flat.

▶ Does the material feel and act like a liquid or a solid?

4 Now scoop up some of the material using both your hands and squeeze it to make a ball. Keep squeezing.

▶ How does it feel?

▶ Is it acting like a liquid or a solid?

5 Next, place the ball of material on the wax paper.

▶ What does it do now?

6 Finally, pour some of the material into a yogurt container. Then gently poke your finger into it.

▶ How is it acting?

Now jab it very hard with your finger.

▶ Does it act like a solid or a liquid?

▶ When does the mystery material behave like a liquid?

▶ What makes it behave like a solid?

(To learn more about this investigation and find the answers to the questions, see pages 20–21.)

Discovery Time

It's fun to investigate liquids and solids in our world.
Now let's check out all the amazing things we've discovered.

What happens to liquids when they are mixed together?

Pages 6–7

When the apple juice was mixed with the blue water, it turned blue. The same thing happened when the blue water was mixed with the milk. However, the oil and blue water did not stay mixed, and the oil didn't turn blue. Instead, the oil and blue water separated. The blue water sank to the bottom of the glass and the oil floated on top of the water. This happened because one of the properties of oil is that it will not mix with water. Also, oil weighs less than water so it floats on water.

Which liquid flows the fastest?

Pages 8–9

The milk is thinnest and has the least viscosity. It flowed fastest and won the race. The cooking oil probably came in second. The ketchup, honey, and shower gel have the most viscosity, so these thicker liquids probably finished behind the milk and oil.

What happens when a liquid gets cold?

Pages 10–11

Every liquid has a freezing point. This is the temperature at which the liquid cools down and turns into a solid. For example, the freezing point of water is 32°F (0°C). In the experiment, the water froze first. The oil probably did not freeze at all. It just became thicker but could still flow. The liquids that did not become solids have a freezing point that is much lower than the freezing point of water. The freezer in your home is not cold enough to turn these liquids into solids.

solid ice

liquid oil

20

What happens to a solid when it's put in water?

The coin, metal fork, sand, and stone sank to the bottom of the bowl. These solids are made of materials that sink in water. The leaf, rubber band, macaroni, and toothpick are made of materials that float in water. Sinking and floating in water are two properties of solids.

Can a solid absorb water?

The kitchen sponge, cotton ball, cardboard, and sock all absorbed water and have the property of being absorbent. The modeling clay, aluminum foil, leaf, and block did not absorb water. These solids have the property of being nonabsorbent.

Can a solid become a liquid?

One of the properties of a solid is its melting point. This is the temperature at which the solid turns into a liquid. The chocolate, butter, and ice cube reached their melting point when they were heated by the hot water. You may even have noticed them starting to melt when you touched them with your warm hands. The eraser, modeling clay, and cheese did not melt. That's because these solids have a much higher melting point. The water was not hot enough to turn these solids into liquids.

Is it a liquid or a solid?

The mystery material is a type of substance that behaves as either a solid or liquid depending upon how much pressure you apply to it. When the mystery material was squeezed or had pressure applied to it, such as your finger jabbing it, the material became a solid and felt hard. When it was in a bowl or yogurt container, or held loosely in your hand, it flowed and could be poured like a liquid.

21

Liquids and Solids in Your World

Now that you've discovered a lot about liquids and solids, check out the ways that you can see liquids and solids in action every day!

1. When you take a bath you might place a plastic toy boat and a bar of soap in the water.

▶ **What happens to each of these solid objects in the water?**

2. After your bath, you use a towel to dry your body and hair.

▶ **What property does a bath towel have that helps you dry off?**

3. A scoop of solid ice cream in a glass of liquid root beer is a tasty treat.

▶ **What happens to the two substances in the glass?**

4. In winter, the temperature can get so cold that liquid water in ponds and puddles becomes solid ice. The fuel that powers cars and buses stays liquid, though.

▶ **Why do you think that is?**

Answers:

1. The solid soap usually passes through the liquid water and sinks to the bottom of the tub. The toy boat floats on the water's surface because it is made of plastic. Plastic is a solid material that has the property of floating on water. 2. A bath towel is absorbent, or absorbs, water. 3. At first, the solid ice cream floats on top of the liquid root beer. As the ice cream gets warm, however, it melts and changes into a liquid. This liquid then mixes with the root beer. 4. Water freezes when the temperature drops to 32°F (0°C). Fuels that power vehicles, such as gas and diesel, are made of oil that has a much lower freezing point than water. If the temperature drops much lower than 32°F (0°C), then these thick liquids may begin to turn lumpy.

22

Science Words

absorb
(ab-ZORB)
to soak up a liquid

flows (FLOHZ) to move in a liquid form; flowing water, for example, might trickle gently from a tap or rush along in a river

liquid (LIK-wid) matter that is neither a solid nor a gas; a liquid flows and changes its shape to fit whatever container it is placed in

predictions
(pri-DIK-shuhnz) guesses that something will happen in a certain way; they are often based on facts a person knows or something a person has observed

properties
(PROP-ur-teez) things you can notice about an object or substance using your senses

solid (SOL-id) matter that is neither a liquid nor a gas; a solid has a definite size and shape

viscosity
(vih-SKOS-ih-tee)
the thickness
of a liquid

23

Index

Read More

Lindeen, Carol K. *Solids, Liquids, and Gases (Nature Basics).* North Mankato, MN: Capstone (2008).

Randolph, Joanne. *Solids in My World (My World of Science).* New York: Rosen (2006).

Taylor-Butler, Christine. *Experiments with Liquids (My Science Investigations).* Chicago: Heinemann (2012).

Learn More Online

To learn more about liquids and solids, visit
www.bearportpublishing.com/FundamentalExperiments

About the Author

Ellen Lawrence lives in the United Kingdom. Her favorite books to write are those about nature and animals. In fact, the first book Ellen bought for herself, when she was six years old, was the story of a gorilla named Patty Cake that was born in New York's Central Park Zoo.